Little Pebble™

Healthy Me

I CARE FOR MY TEETH

by Martha E. H. Rustad

Raintree is an imprint of Capstone Global Library Limited, a company incorporated in England and Wales having its registered office at 264 Banbury Road, Oxford, OX2 7DY – Registered company number: 6695582

www.raintree.co.uk
myorders@raintree.co.uk

Edited by Shelly Lyons
Designed by Juliette Peters
Picture research by Jo Miller
Production by Tori Abraham

ISBN 978 1 4747 3487 5 (hardback)
20 19 18 17 16
10 9 8 7 6 5 4 3 2 1

ISBN 978 1 4747 3491 2 (paperback)
21 20 19 18 17
10 9 8 7 6 5 4 3 2 1

British Library Cataloguing in Publication Data
A full catalogue record for this book is available from the l

Acknowledgements
Images by Capstone Studio: Karon Dubke
Photo Styling: Sarah Schuette and Marcy Morin

Every effort has been made to contact copyright holders of material reproduced in this book. Any omissions will be rectified in subsequent printings if notice is given to the publisher.

All the Internet addresses (URLs) given in this book were valid at the time of going to press. However, due to the dynamic nature of the Internet, some addresses may have changed, or sites may have changed or ceased to exist since publication. While the author and publisher regret any inconvenience this may cause readers, no responsibility for any such changes can be accepted by either the author or the publisher.

Printed and bound in India.

Contents

Brush!

Smile!

I want healthy teeth.

I brush my teeth twice a day.

I brush for two minutes.

I brush every tooth.

I floss.

I get the plaque out!

Food and drinks

I eat healthy food.

Milk keeps my teeth strong.

Yum!

I drink water.

Fizzy drinks hurt my teeth.

I brush my teeth after
eating sweets.
If I can't brush, I rinse
with water.
Swish!

The dentist

I go to the dentist's surgery.

She cleans my teeth.

I get a new toothbrush.

The dentist checks my mouth.

He looks at X-rays

of my teeth.

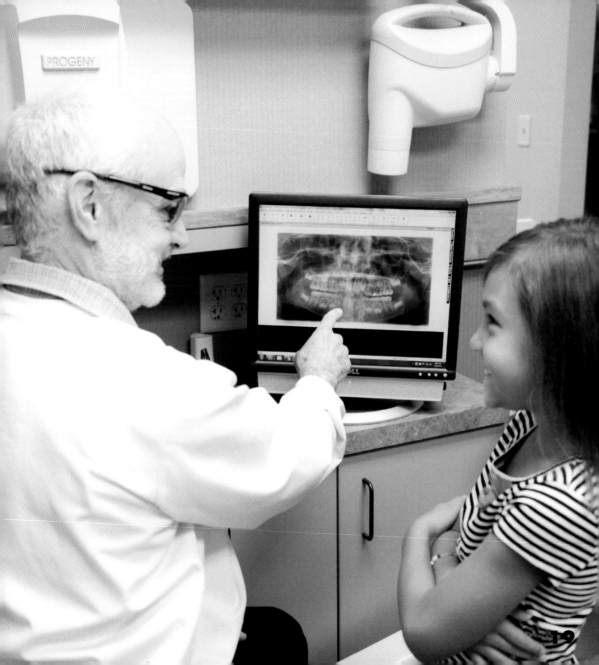

I look after my teeth.

Healthy teeth are part

of a healthy me!

Glossary

dentist person that takes care of teeth

floss to clean between teeth with a thin string

healthy fit and well; good for you

plaque a build-up on teeth that causes teeth to decay and rot

rinse to wash with clean water

X-ray a picture that looks inside your body; an X-ray of a mouth shows the roots of teeth

Find out more

Books

Going to the Dentist, Roderick Hunt (OUP, 2012)

Looking After Your Teeth (Take Care of Yourself), Sian Smith (Raintree, 2013)

Teeth (Looking After Me), Liz Grogerly (Wayland, 2012)

Websites

kidshealth.org/en/kids/go-dentist.html
Find out more about what happens when you visit the dentist.

www.bbc.co.uk/northernireland/schools/4_11/topteeth/
Discover fun games to help you remember how to take care of your teeth.

www.childrensuniversity.manchester.ac.uk/interactives/science/teethandeating/lookingafter/
Find interactive tips for keeping your teeth healthy

Comprehension questions

1. You should brush your teeth for how many minutes?

2. Why do you think it is good to drink milk?

3. A dentist looks at X-rays. What are X-rays?

Index